POLAND

Lithuania

Berlorussia

AŁKI

STÓW

STOK

Wieprz

LUBLIN

ZAMOŚĆ

SANDOMIERZ

San

MYŚL

ANOK

ZCZADY

Ukraine

Photography by: Stanisława, Jolanta and Rafał Jabłoński

Text by Rafał Jabłoński

Graphic design by Rafał Jabłoński

ISBN 83-909878-5-6

Published by Festina SC , Warsaw, tel/fax (+48) (22) 842-54-53

Warsaw 2005

Poland, a Central European country situated between the major powers, Russian and Germany, has had a turbulent 1,000-year history.

Pre-Slavonic and Slavonic tribes already began settling these lands in the 15th century BC. Prehistoric evidence has been provided by,

꙰ The landscape in the vicinity of Karpacz.

among other things, excavations at the site of a prehistoric settlement of the Lusatian culture in Biskupin, dating from c. 550 BC. Among the tribes inhabiting those areas in the 9th century AD were the Polanians, whose capital was Gniezno, and the Vistulians with their capital in Kraków or Wiślica. The Polanian state's Piast Dynasty conquered neighbouring tribes, includ-

ing the Vistulians, and began consolidating Slavonic lands. A turning point in the annals of Polish statehood was the acceptance of Christianity by Duke Mieszko I. That act occurred in 966 and brought Poland into the realm of Latin culture, thereby averting Poland's conversion 'by fire and sword' as a pagan country. Mieszko's successor, Bolesław I the Brave, brought

6

about the creation of a Christian bishopric in Gniezno and exploited the martyr's death of Bishop Wojciech, a missionary killed while trying to convert the pagan Prussians, for propaganda purposes. He could then strive to elevate the Christian nation Poland had become to the rank of a kingdom. He accomplished that feat in 1025, when be became the first crowned king of Poland. In 1039, his successor, Casimir the Renewer, moved his capital to Kraków, which for centuries to come would be the centre of Poland's political and social life. The last representative of the Piast Dynasty was Casimir the Great, of which it has been said that 'he

For storks, Poland is one of Europe's biggest nesting areas.

Haying time in the village of Ząb in the Podhale area.

found a Poland built of wood and left behind one built of brick and stone'. Following his heirless death, his nephew Louis of Hungary ascended the throne. His daughter Jadwiga married the Grand Duke of Lithuania, Jagiełło, and that marriage sealed a un

» A cart from horse-carts museum in Łańcut.

-- Zygmunt the Old and Zygmunt August -- has come to be known as 'the golden age'. Following Zygmunt August's heirless death up till 1795, Poland was ruled by elected monarchs, chosen by the entire gentry in the Election Fields of the town of Wola outside Warsaw. The way the kings were elected often led to elections unfavourable to

˅ A glimpse of the primeval forests near Augustów.

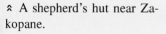

˄ A shepherd's hut near Zakopane.

ion between Poland and Lithuania creating the Jagiellonian Dynasty that reigned until 1572. That was an exceptionally good period for Poland. The reign of that dynasty's last kings

8

Poland's raison d'état. Rather than the good of the country, the primary concern were the interests of the gentry who over time obtained growing privileges, thereby weakening royal authority and the state. A practical reflection of that state of affairs was the 'nihil novi' constitution of 1505, which made any decisions affecting the gentry impossible without their consent. Another was the privilege known as 'liberum veto' - 'I do not permit', which enabled a nobleman to adjourn parliament with a single dissenting vote. The first elected monarch, Henri de Valois (Henryk Walezy), fled to France after a short reign. But the throne also

⌄ House-to-house carollers in the village of Żabnica in the Beskid Żywiecki Mountains.

⌃ Hundred-year-old oaks in Rogalin park near Poznań.

got entrusted to outstanding individuals. Among them were Stefan Batory, Jan III Sobieski and Stanisław August Poniatowski. From 1587 to 1668 Poland was ruled by the Vasa Dynasty of Swedish origin, and after the death of Jan III Sobieski, the Wittin Dynasty of Saxony came to power, represented by August II and August III. In the 17th and 18th century Poland declined in importance, and that led to the first partition in which Russia, Austria and Prussia annexed nearly 30% of its territory. At that time, attempts were undertaken to introduce reforms, whose most eloquent manifestation was the Constitution of 3 May 1791. But its provisions were annulled by the traitorous Confederation of Targowica, and in 1793 Poland was partitioned a second time. The third partition, carried out in 1795, wiped Poland off the map of Europe for 123 years. Poland only regained its independence on the basis of the Treaty of Versailles after the First World War. Unfortunately, not for long. In September 1939, the Republic of Poland was invaded by Germany and the USSR. Throughout the entire Second World War Poles fought against the Nazi occupation forces at home and abroad. After the war, a new geopolitical order established at Yalta would make Poland dependent on the Soviet Union for the next 45 years. The Polish nation's numerous revolts against communist rule (1956, 1970, 1976) were quashed by force. It was only the strikes by workers affiliated with the Solidarity trade union lea

ded by Lech Wałęsa that led to a change of Poland's political system and the country's full sovereignty. On 31 December 1989, the Third Polish Republic was born.

Kurpie. Corpus Christi procession.

An old piece of farm machinery in a field near Warsaw.

LITTLE POLAND

Little Poland in the 9th century was the area belonging to the tribal state of the Vistulians with its capital in Kraków or Wiślica. Subjugated by the Polanians during the reign of King Casimir the Renewer, it became Poland's most important region. In 1039, the capital of Poland was moved to Kraków. Little Poland (Małopolska) is a region abounding in architectural relics and splendid scenery. Folk traditions are also cultivated there.

» Shepherd's huts in the Tatra Mountains' Kościelisko Valley.

˅ Each year on the first Thursday of December a Christmas crèche contest is held round the Adam Mickiewicz Monument. These colourful creations incorporate elements of Kraków's architectural treasures.

» The Murowaniec Hostel of the PTTK (Polish Tourism and Sightseeing Society) was built in the Hala Gąsienicowa mountain pasture in 1925 according to the design of Jan Kalinowski. Built of granite blocks hewn from local rock formations, it can accommodate 100 guests and has a dining-room and food service. The hostel's overriding principle, like that of other hostels in the Tatra Mountains, is to accept every weary traveller.

» The Tatra Mountains are the ideal place to engage in winter sports. The principal ski-lifts are found on the slopes of Kasprowy Wierch in the Gąsienica and Goryczka mountain pastures.

⌄ The Chapel of Our Lady of Perpetual Help, erected atop Mount Gubałówka in 1967, is an example of the timber architecture typical of the Podhale region.

⌄ Throngs of tourists flock to the Tatra Mountains each year. Dozens of tourist trails with a total length of 250 kilometres await them.

Lake Morskie Oko (Eye of the Sea) and the higher-lying Czarny Staw (Black Pond) are the Tatras' most beautiful mountain lakes -- relics of the glacial era. The glacial pothole containing lake Morskie Oko is closed off by a moraine, atop which a mountain hostel has been built. The lake is surrounded by tall peaks such as Opalony, Miedziane, Zabie and Mnich.

⌃ Zakopane, situated at the foot of the Tatra Mountains, is Poland's winter capital. As late as the mid-19th century it was still a forgotten hamlet. Thanks to the interests of the romantics in nature, it became a well-known resort.

« In Jaszczurówka near Zakopane stands a wooden chapel designed by Stanisław Witkiewicz, the creator of the Zakopane style. It was built in 1908.

» Krupówki street, Zakopane's main promenade, ranks among Poland's most famous streets. Polyglot throngs of tourists intermingle with the highland folklore of horse-drawn fourwheelers.

» The cemetery at Pęskowy Brzysk is one of Poland's best-known graveyards. Established in 1850, it is the final resting place of many personalities associated with the town.

˅ Atma Villa, built in the 'Zakopane style' in 1892, houses the museum of the renowned Polish composer, Karol Szymanowski.

» Established in the 16th century, the village of Chochołów is known for its historic timber cottages facing the road and stretching the length of the village.

⌄ One of Poland's most beautiful wooden country churches is found in the village of Orawka. It was built in 1650-1652. It contains an organ dating from c. 1670 and its interior is decorated with polychromy from c. 1711.

« Chochołów Valley, the biggest Tatra Mountain valley, leads to Chochołów Clearing with the shepherd huts once used by highlanders tending their sheep and cattle.

⌄ In the village of Ząb near the town of Poronin, traditional highland attire is cultivated and can be admired during processions held on Corpus Christi.

⌃ The timber church in Rabka was built in 1606. At present, it houses the Władysław Orkan Memorial Regional Museum.

⌄ Orawa Ethnographic Park in Zubrzyca Górna was set up in 1955. Many examples of folk art from the Orawa and Podhale areas have been assembled there.

18

» ˅ The wooden church of St Michael the Archangel in Dębno has survived nearly intact since the latter half of the 15th century. Its walls and ceilings are decorated with vintage-1500 polychromy. Resembling a fabric, the design features more than 70 motifs, including a rider, animals, plants, St. George fighting a dragon and halbardiers.

˅ The painting entitled 'The Holy Family' from 1516 is found in St Ann's Church in Nowy Targ.

» This early-Gothic church in the village of Frydmann is the oldest relic of religious architecture in the Tatra northern foothills.

⌃   In the village of Łopuszna in picturesque Gorczańska Valley stands the family manor of the Tetmajers. Next door to it stands what is known as the Klemens Cottage with accompanying out-buildings. The manor houses a Museum of Gentry Culture.

» The timber church in Ło-puszna standing on the bank of the River Dunajec was built round the turn of the 16th century. It has a front tower with slanting walls.

˅ The Dunajec flows through the Pieniny Mountains through a winding, picturesque canyon. Tourists may travel the stretch of the river between Sromowce Niżne and Szczawnica aboard rafts.

˅» The Pieniny are a mountain chain situated to the south-west of Nowy Targ. Trzy Korony (Three Crowns) Peak (982 metres above sea-level) towers above the Dunajec in the Czorsztyn Pieniny.

˅ The castle in Niedzica was built on an escarpment overlooking the River Dunajec for the Berzevicsy Family some time before 1330. It has towered above the waters of Lake Czorsztyn ever since that artificial lake was created.

» On a limestone cliff overlooking Lake Czorsztyn stands Czorsztyn Castle. In was built in stages during the 14th and 15th centuries, but fell into ruin atfer 1795.

» Lake Solińskie is a 21-square-kilometre body of water formed by the damming-up of the River San. It is Poland's biggest artificial lake. Many holiday localities are found along its shores including Solina and Polańczyk.

« Krynica has developed as a health resort since 1793 when Franciszek Stic von Saunbergen began building the first pump-house. The Old Pump-House, erected in 1889, is Krynica's most interesting architectural relic.

« The former Eastern Orthodox Church of St Paraxevia was built in Kwiatoń in 1700. It is a wooden church divided into three parts, each of which is topped by a steeple.

» The Bieszczady are a mountain range stretching across the south-eastern corner of the country. Bieszczady National Park was established to protect the local flora and fauna.

» Neo-Gothic Jordan Palace, built in 1905, is a familiar landmark in Olszanica along the road between Sanok and Ustrzyki Dolne. Situated on an island, it nestles in a picturesque park.

≳ The timber former Eastern Orthodox church in Certeź, now a Catholic church, was built in 1742. An onion dome crowns its central section.

« The Eastern Orthodox church in the village of Skwirtne from 1837 is a typical Lemko church in the north-western style. It is characterised by a three-part plan comprising three quadrangles with a nave that is always wider. Individual parts of the building are at different levels and the towers are domed.

The Skansen in Sanok is the biggest museum of its kind in Poland. It contains a collection of structures reflecting the folk architecture of five ethnographic groups: the Boikos, Lemkos, Dolinians (valley-dwellers), inhabitants of Eastern Podgórze (Piedmont) and Western Podgórze. Included are Eastern Orthodox and Catholic country churches, entire peasant farmsteads and wayside shrines.

» Rzeszów Castle was built at the turn of the 17th century for the aristocratic House of Lubomirski. The present structure was erected in the 20th century on the flame-gutted remains of its predecessor. Only an 18th-century tower has survived.

˅ Krasiczyn Castle was erected in the years 1592-1618 for the Krasicki family. Marcin Krasicki transformed it into a residence, with architect Galeazzo Appiani overseeing the project.

« The fortified Greek Catholic Church of St Humphrey in Posada Rybotycka is the oldest Orthodox-type church in Poland. It was built at the turn of the 15th century, and its defensive tower was added in 1506.

˅ The Church of the Annunciation of the Blessed Virgin Mary in Leżajsk dates from 1618-1628. Inside is a famous organ from 1680-1693, known for its exceptionally rich carved decorations. A curious feature are such special sound effects as the chirping of birds.

˅ The most noteworthy architectural relic in Jarosław is the Renaissance dwelling-house of the Orsetti merchant family. Built in c. 1581, it underwent alterations in the 17th century. A crested attic is the building's crowning touch, and arcades clearly enhance its charm. At present, it houses a regional museum.

⌃ ⌄ Łańcut Castle was built in the period from 1629 to 1641 for Stanisław Lubomirski. After 1775, Izabella Lubomirska commissioned Chrystian Piotr Aigner to redesign the castle into a palatial residence.

⌄ Today Łańcut Castle houses a museum of interiors. In its classicist Hall of Columns stands a late-18th-century statue of Cupid, sculpted by Antonio Canova.

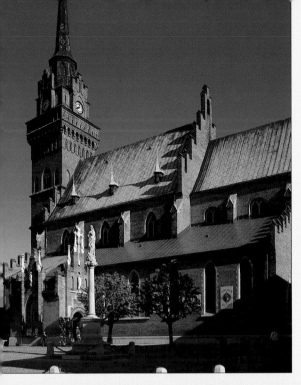

« The Gothic cathedral of the Nativity of the Blessed Virgin Mary in Tarnów dates from 1400. The main nave's ceiling displays 16th-century net vaulting. Numerous neo-Gothic fragments date from a 19th-century expansion scheme.

⌃ The Tarnów marketplace is surrounded by dwelling-houses, some of which were built during the Renaissance period. The 14th-century town hall was redesigned in the latter half of the 16th century.

« Tarnów Cathedral contains many superb cultural relics, The most valuable of them are the tombstones along its walls. One of them is that of the Family Ostrogski, owners of the town from the Tarnowski line. The Ostrogski tombstone was created in 1606-1620 by sculptor Jan Pfister.

The timber cemetery church of St Leonard in Lipnica Murowana dates from the end of the 15th century. Gothic and Renaissance polychromy adorns its interior.

˅ A Corpus Christi procession in Lipnica Murowana.

≽ The parish church of Corpus Christi in Biecz, built at the turn of the 16th century, is an example of how the new Renaissance style influenced late Gothic architecture.

« The castle in Wiśnicz had originally belonged to the Kmita Family and later became the property of the Lubomirskis. It was built in the first half of the 16th century. The structure's renovation was carried out in 1615-1621 by Maciej Trapola.

The village of Zalipie is known for its colourfully painted cottages. Since 1948, two days after the Feast of Corpus Christi, an annual conterst is held in which the villagers participate.

⋩ A Benedictine abbey, founded in c. 1070 by King Bolesław the Bold, is found in Tyniec atop a 40-metre rock formation overlooking a bend in the Vistula.

⋩ In 1940 in Oświęcim (Auschwitz), the Nazi Germans set up their biggest extermination camp in Poland. All told, some 1,5 million people perished there. The concentration camp had been originally intended for Poles, but the Germans soon began bringing in people from all over Europe, and from 1942 it became the biggest camp exterminating Jews. Father Maksymilian Kolbe, a Catholic priest, died in Auschwitz, sacrificing his life for that of another prisoner. In the former Auschwitz barracks an exhibition showing the camp's history may be seen. A ramp onto which prisoners were unloaded and where the selection process took place has survived in nearby Birkenau.

The salt-mine in Wieliczka has been included on UNESCO's World Cultural Heriatge List. Its oldest shaft dates from 1280. Many of its chambers have been adorned with rock-salt sculptures.

⌃ The pilgrimage-shrine complex in Kalwaria Zebrzydowska
has attracted worshippers for
nearly four centuries. During
Holy Week it is the scene of
a passion play culminating on
Easter Sunday. The Baroque
church and Bernardine monastery were built in 1604-1617.

» Ojców National Park encom-
passes the picturesque valley of
the River Prądnik. There is
found the Gothic-Renaissance
castle in Pieskowa Skała, built
by King Casimir the Great. Of
great interest are the numerous,
fantastically shaped rock formations in the vicinity, including
the famous Hercules' Club.

« St Mary's Church in Kraków was funded by Kraków burghers. Its construction began in 1355 and lasted till the early 16th century.

˅ St Andrew's Church and the Cloister of the Poor Clares along Kraków's Royal Way were founded by the Palatine Sieciech and built in 1079-1098. As one of the oldest churches in Kraków, it has retained its Romanesque appearance, and only its interior was transformed during a Baroque-style renovation around 1700.

« The stained-glass window 'God the Father' from 1904 in the Franciscan Church.

≽ At the centre of the Kraków marketplace is a drapers' hall known as Sukiennice. The hall was built round merchants' stalls in the mid-14th century. Following a fire in 1555, the structure was rebuilt in the Renaissance style.

≽ The Collegium Maius Building, the seat of the Jagiellonian University, was erected towards the close of the 15th century and patterned on Italian architecture.

» The parade led by the 'Zwierzyniec Pony', known as the Lajkonik, starts on the Octave of Corpus Christi from the Cloister of the Norbertine Sisters in Kraków. It commemorates the repulsion of a Tartar attack in 1287. The costume used today was designed by Stanisław Wyspiański in 1905.

≈ Kraków's Wawel Cathedral of SS Wenceslaus and Stanislaus was founded in the 14th century by King Władysław the Short. The cathedral was the scene of royal coronations and the burial place of Poland's kings.

« The Confession of St Stanislaus occupies a central place in Wawel Cathedral where the nave and the transept meet. The remains of St Florian were enshrined in that mausoleum in 1184 and those of St Stanislaus -- in 1254. The confession's present form was created in 1626-1629 thanks to the patronage of Bishop Marcin Szyszkowski. The project was carried out by royal architect Jan Trevani, and the standing figures of Poland's patron saints were the work of Antoni Lagostini. The coffin adorned with scenes from the life of St Francis was created in the Gdańsk workshop of Piotr van der Rennan in 1669-1671.

⌃ King Zygmunt's Chapel in Kraków's Wawel Cathedral was founded by King Zygmunt the Old and built in 1519-1531. Poland's most exquisite work of Renaissance art was created by Italian architect Bartłomiej Berecci.

« The tombstone of King Casimir Jagiellonian in Wawel Cathedral was sculpted in red marble by Wit Stwosz round the close of the 15th century.

« The Royal Castle on Kraków's Wawel Hill was the residence of the Piast, Jagiellonian and Vasa Dynasties. At that site, a Romanesque palace cum rotunda was built at the turn of the 11th century. The royal residence received its present Renaissance form in the years 1502-1536. The castle's wings are enclosed by a superb arcaded courtyard.

« The name of Wawel Castle's Tournament Hall came from the motif of a frieze running below the ceiling. Its autor was Hans Dürer, brother of the renowned Albrecht Dürer.

⌄ The mannerist-Baroque Camedulian monastic complex, built in Kraków's Bielany quarter in 1605-1642, was founded by Andrzej Wolski.

⌄ The Deputies' Hall in Wawel Castle features a coffered ceiling containing sculpted human heads. They were the creation of Jan Janda and Sebastian Tauerbach of Wrocław in the mid-15th century.

» Niepołomice Castle east of Kraków was erected during the reign of King Casimir the Great in the mid-14th century. The renovation carried out in 1550-1571 transformed it into a royal residence. Its pride is a Renaissance gate from 1552.

The Kraków-Częstochow a Upland comprises low limestone rock formations from the Jurassic period. Karst-type phenomena are responsible for their unusual shapes.

The ruins of Ogrodzieniec Castle are found in the village of Podzamcze in the Kraków-Częstochowa Jura. The Renaissance structure was erected in 1530-1545 for Kraków burgher Maćko Borkowic.

The ruins of a Gothic castle in Mirów are the remains of a structure dating from the times of Casimir the Great. It comprises an upper castle with a defensive tower and a lower castle with a residential tower and courtyard.

« The royal castle in Bobolice was built in the first half of the 14th century. Today's ruins reveals the castle's oval outline and a cylindrical and semi-cylindrical tower.

» The ruins of a castle built before 1349 by Casimir the Great are found on a limestone rock in Olsztyn near Częstochowa. All that has survived are fragments of its bastions, walls and tower.

The Pauline Monastery at Jasna Góra (Bright Mountain) in Częstochowa was established on the basis of a decree issued by its founder, Prince Władysław of Opole, in 1382. The first Gothic structures went up in the 15th century. The oldest part of the Chapel of the Blessed Virgin dates from that period. However, most of the buildings were erected in the 17th century. The church received its Baroque interior after a fire in 1690.

» The Chapel of our Lady of Częstochowa contains a miraculous painting of Byzantine or Italian origin -- Poland's most sacred Catholic icon.

≽ The sacristy of the Pauline monastery at Jasna Góra, built in 1649-1651, contains painted decorations executed by Karol Dankwart after 1690.

⌃ The treasury of the Jasna Góra Monastery contains the most valuable gifts given to the monastery by pilgrims. They include chasubles, liturgical vessels, jewellery and national mementoes. Amongst them is a reliquary cross donated by King Zygmunt the Old in 1510.

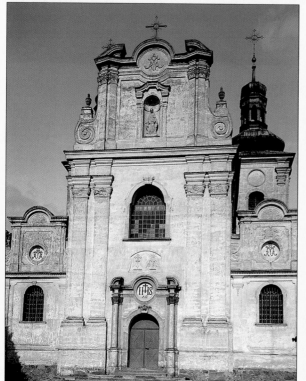

⌃ Chęciny Castle was built before 1306 by Kraków Bishop Jan Muskata. It was later enlarged by Kings Władysław the Short and Casimir the Great. It has lain in ruins since the 17th-century Swedish invasion.

The name of the Benedictine monastery at Święty Krzyż (Holy Cross) comes from the relics of the Christ's Cross enshrined there since 1723. The paintings of Franciszek Smuglewicz adorn its classicist interior.

⌃ Treeless swaths formed from quartz rock and Cambrian shells may be seen running through forested areas on the slopes of the Łysa Góra and Łysica mountain.

Baranów Castle was erected in 1591-1606 on the site of a former manor. This Renaissance residence was believed to have been designed by Santi Gucci for Andrzej Leszczyński. The internal courtyard is surrounded on three sides by one-storey-tall arcaded and columned galleries. On the entrance side is a curtain wall with a staircase extending into the courtyard.

⌃ In the 9th century, Sandomierz on the Vistula was one of Poland's three main castle towns, the others being Kraków and Wrocław. The most interesting structure in its marketplace is the 14th-century town hall which took on its Renaissance appearance during a 16th-century renovation project.

« Queen Hedwig's Ravine in Sandomierz is the most beautiful loessic ravine in the area. It is 500 metres long with steep 10-metre walls. Its slopes are thickly overgrown with trees and shrubs, of which the legally protected dwarf cherry is especially noteworthy.

» The Cathedral of the Nativity of the Blessed Virgin Mary in Sandomierz dates from the times of Casimir the Great. The Gothic church was erected on the relics of a Romanesque one in stages beginning in 1350. In the presbytery are found Byzantiune-Ruthenian pictures founded by King Władysław Jagiełło.

⚹ Sandomierz Cathedral abounds in Rococo sculptures decorating the altars set up next to pillars between naves.

⚹ Góry Pieprzowe (Pepper Hills) to the north of Sandomierz were formed from slate and quartzite some 500 million years old. Exposed to the elements, those rocks crumble and create rubble whose colour gave the hills their name. The hills are pock-marked with little hollows which gives them their distinct appearance.

« Lublin's most valuable architectural relic is Holy Trinity Chapel dating from the 14th century and situated in the castle courtyard. The interior is adorned with Rutheno-Byzantine frescoes founded by King Władysław Jagiełło.

» Lublin's 14th-century castle was completely destroyed. On that site, a prison in the English Gothic style was built in 1824-1826.

⌃ Zamość, known as the 'Padua of the north', was designed by Italian architect Bernardo Morando according to the Renaissance vision of 'the ideal town'. Construction began in 1581, when Zamość was owned by chancellor and great crown hetman Jan Zamoyski. The town hall was built in the late 16th century according to B. Morando's design.

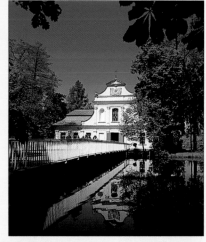

↲ Roztocze National Park is traversed by the Rivers Wieprz and Tanew. A low waterfall known as 'the roars' is found along the Tanew.

» The Church of St John Nepomucene in Zwierzyniec is situated on a picturesque island. It was built in 1741-1747 according the design of Jerzy de Kawe.

« A peasant farmstead from the turn of the 20th century is found in Gu-ciów on Wieprz. It comprisses a peasant cottage, two out-buildings and cattle sheds. The interior has been fitted with rustic utensils of the period.

SILESIA

Silesia which originally belonged to Bohemia, came under the reign of the Piast princes in c. 990. Later it was ruled by Czechs, Austrians and Prussians. The region is divided into Upper Silesia, whose capital is Katowice, and Lower Silesia, whose principle city is Wrocław.

» The Sudeten ridge is a popular winter-sports area. Such localities as Karpacz and Szklarska Poręba offer numerous ski-lifts.

˅ Folk traditions are cultivated in Koniaków in the Beskid Żywiecki Mountains. An exhibition of lace is found in the home of Maria Gwarkowa, and at the folk-art gallery the creations of local artists may be admired.

« Gliwice's high street, Aleja Zwycięstwa (Victory Avenue), leads to the town square. It is lined by numerous dwelling-houses displaying elaborate Secession décor.

⌃ The Fountain of the Dancing Fauns was built in Gliwice in the early 19th century by Teodor Kalida.

« A fortified castle from the times of King Casimir the Great stands in Będzin overlooking the River Czarna Przemsza. It is surrounded by a double ring of defensive walls.

⌃ To get from the Pszczyna marketplace to the castle one must pass through the 17th-century Gate of the Chosen Ones. The formerly Gothic ducal palace was erected in the years 1870-1875 according to the French Renaissance design of Alexander Destailleur.

⌃ The Grand Salon of Pszczyna Castle is the most magnificent room in this museum of interiors. The scenes of Dirck Dalens II have been set in splendid wood panelling. The Salon is joined to the Library by a wide passageway.

» A lion sculpture in front of Pszczyna Castle.

⌃ Brzeg Castle was built in the Renaissance style in 1538-1560. Worthy of particular note is its arcaded courtyard, designed in 1541-1560 by J. and F. Parr, who patterned it after that of Kraków's Wawel Castle. The Renaissance gatehouse surprises tourists with its ornate sculpted décor. Statues of Prince Jerzy II and Princess Barbara keep their silent vigil over the gate, and above them stretches a row of stone busts of the Silesian Piasts and rulers of Poland.

« Mural paintings of biblical scenes adorn the walls of the Parish Church of St John the Apostle in Małujowice dating from the early 15th century. The ceiling is covered with pictures applied through the use of stencils cut out of leather.

» The castle in Moszna was built to reflect the style of Elisabethan castles.

» The Church of the Assumption of the Blessed Virgin Mary and St John the Baptist as well as the Cistercian Monastery in Henryków were built in 1241.

˅ In front of St Anne's Church in Sobótka stands an oddity popularly known as 'the mushroom' or 'monk's body'. It is the lower part of a granite statue dating from pre-Christian times.

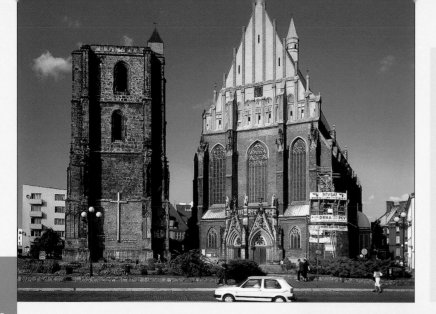

The Church of SS James and Agnes in Nysa was built in 1423-1430 by the Silesian architect Piotr of Ząbkowice. A beautiful portal adorns its main entrance.

⮛ Renaissance and Baroque-style houses stand in Bracka street as well as in the marketplace and adjoining streets of Nysa. In front of them is Tryton's Fountain. In the background is seen the superb Baroque Church of Saints Peter and Paul, built in 1720-1727 by architects Feliks Anton Scheffer and Thomas Scheffer. The vaulting of the single-nave church was adorned with illusionistic painting in 1930. Next to it stands the former monastery of the Monks of the Holy Sepulchre in which a theological seminary is now housed.

» The Church of SS Nicholas and Francis Xavier in Otmuchów, a church of the galleried-basilica type, was built in 1706-1707. Galleries are located above its chapels.

⚹ The Parish Church of the Assumption of the Blessed Virgin Mary in Kłodzko was built in stages from 1344 to 1555. It is a Gothic, three-nave basilica with stellar and net vaulting. Its 17th-century renovation was responsible for the church's Baroque décor. Earlier art works have also survived: in the main altar a statue of Our Lady of Kłodzko from c. 1450 and the figure of Our Lady with a Finch from about 1350. In 1665-1690 a Jesuit monastery was built onto the church.

↵ In the Baroque Church of the Visitation of the BVM in Bardo there is a reputedly miraculous figure of the Blessed Virgin and Infant, known as the Enthroned Madonna. It is believed to be the oldest sculpture in Silesia.

⌃ The rich Baroque interior décor of the Parish Church of St Bartholomew in Głogówek was the work of two artists: painter Franciszek Sebastini and stucco artist Jan Schubert.

« The Chapel of Skulls is found at Czermna within the town limits of Kudowa Zdrój. In 1776, the local parish priest collected the remains of those fallen in battle as well as plague victims and used them to line the walls of his church. He managed to gather 3,000 skulls and shin bones.

» Known as 'the Silesian Jerusalem', the Shrine in Wambierzyce was built in the years from 1683 to 1725. The Church of the Visitation of the Bblessed Virgin Mary is a basilica in the style of the Italian Renaissance.

⌃ The Table Mountains are one of Lower Silesia's leading tourist attractions. Their cracked and weathered sandstone has created unusual rock formations resembling mushrooms, columns and gates. The highest peak, Great Szczeliniec, rises to a height of 919 metres above sea level. The best-known rock formations are Little Szczeliniec, Errant Rocks and Rocky Mushrooms. Those mountains are almost entirely covered with thick forests.

Already in the Middle Ages, a castle had stood on a rocky escarpment in Książ near Wałbrzych. Following numerous renovations, including the incorporation of Renaissance and Baroque elements, the building was given its present eclectic appearance in the early 20th century.

»↴ The Church of the Assumption of the Blessed Virgin Mary in Krzeszów, built in 1728-1735, is a pearl of Silesian Baroque.

≽ At Legnickie Pole in 1241, Polish forces clashed with the invading Tartars, and Prine Henryk II the Pious fell in battle. The local Church of St Hedwig, dating from 1727-1731, ranks among Silesia's most magnificent examples of Baroque architecture.

« Czocha Castle stands atop a tall escarpment overlooking an artificial lake created in 1900-1905. Originally built as a 13th-century Lusatian stronghold, it underwent renovation projects in the 16th, 17th and 20th centuries.

Granite, crystalline shells and gneiss constitute the rock structure of the Karkonosze Mountains. Many granite rock formations there have assumed fantastic shapes. Glacier activity was responsible for leaving fields of rock rubble such as that on Mount Śnieżka as well as potholes containing picturesque little lakes.

» In Karpacz at the foot of the Karkonosze Mountains stands Poland's oldest, wooden, Romanesque house of worship, the Church of Wang. Built in the 13th century in the south of Norway in the locality of Wang, it was purchased by Frederick Wilhelm IV, disassembled and transported first to Berlin and later to Karpacz, where it was re-assembled in 1842-1843. A stone tower was added on at that time.

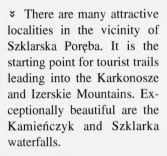

˅ There are many attractive localities in the vicinity of Szklarska Poręba. It is the starting point for tourist trails leading into the Karkonosze and Izerskie Mountains. Exceptionally beautiful are the Kamieńczyk and Szklarka waterfalls.

» Ostrów Tumski (Cathedral Islet) and Piasek (Sand) Islet are where the history of Wrocław began. Pictured is 13th-century Holy Cross Church and the Archcathedral.

« Wrocław's old town hall is the city's most splendid example of secular mediaeval architecture. Built between 1327 and 1510, its façade displays striking, typically Gothic décor.

» The Library of the Osslolinński National Institute is housed in the building of a former crusaders' monastery. The building was constructed in 1675-1715. Collections of drawings and old prints, moved after the war from Lwów, are stored there.

« The Hansel and Gretel houses in the Wrocław marketplace are the last of more than a dozen houses once inhabited by acolytes and canons of St Elisabeth's Church.

« The most exquisite hall of Wrocław University is the Aula Leopoldina dating from 1728-1741. This pearl of the Baroque fascinates visitors with its rich, iconographically complex décor.

GREAT POLAND

Great Poland was the cradle of Polish statehood. In the mid-9th century the Polanians, the mightiest of the Slavonic tribes, built their state in that region and imposed their supremacy on neighbouring tribes. The first two Polish capitals -- Gniezno and Poznań -- were in Great Poland.

» A landscape in the vicinity of Poznań.

˅ Osieczna's main claim to fame are its three old windmills situated along the road to Leszno. They were built in the latter half of the 18th century.

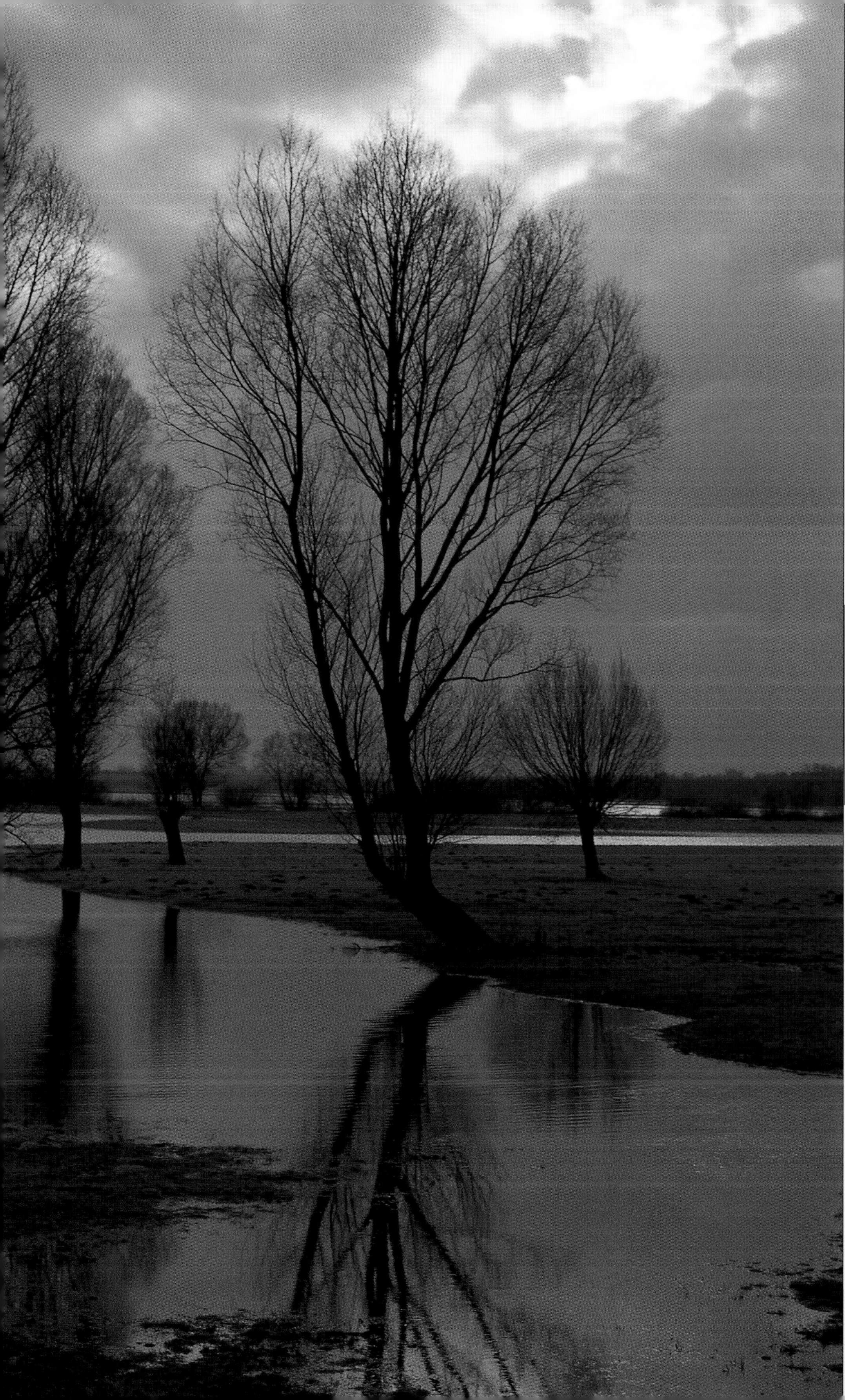

« Poznań, which lies along the River Warta, is the historic capital of Great Poland. Its main architectural relic is the late-13th-century town hall, later enlarged in the Renaissance style by Giovanni B. Quadro. At noon, high atop its tower, two mechancial butting goats appear.

ⱴ The Baroque-style Church of St Stanislaus was erected over the period from 1651 to 1732.

68

» The National Museum of Poznań is housed in a building built in 1900-1903 originally as the Emperor Frederick III Prussian Memorial Museum. The museum contains masterpieces of Polish and foreign painting. It includes the biggest collection of Jacek Malczewski's paintings as well as works by the outstanding Dutch artists Quentin Maasis and Joos van Cleve. Seen in the photograph is Vlastimil Hofmann's Madonna.

✿ The monumental Gothic cathedral of SS Peter and Paul towers above Ostrów Tumski (Cathedral Islet). In its golden chapel, built in the Byzantine style in 1834-1841, the remains of Mieszko I and Bolesław the Brave have been laid to rest.

✿ Poznań's Raczyński Library was built in the style of French classicism in 1821-1828.

» The bee-hive museum is found in Swarzędz, a locality renowned for its manufacture of furniture. It was set up at the Institute for the Research of Insect Diseases.

⌃ This Baroque-style manor housein Koszuty with its stucco-covered timber-pole walls and shingled sloping roof was built round the end of the 18th century for Józef Zabłocki. At present it houses the Środa Area Museum.

« Tytus Działyński commissioned Karl Schinkel to design neo-Gothic Kórnik Castle. It is situated on an island and surrounded by a romantic scenic park.

» Classicist Śmielów Palace was designed by the well-known Warsaw architect Stanisław Zawadzki. Built in 1797, it once played host to Poland's great romantic bard, Adam Mickiewicz.

⅋ The castle in Gołuchów in its present Renaissance form emerged in 1872-1885. Its owner, Elżbieta Działyńska, created there one of Poland's first private museums.

⅋ Construction of rococo-classicist Rogalin Palace for Kazimierz Raczyński began in 1770. In 1782-1783 a semicircular gallery ending with annexes was built on, giving the palace a more modern, classicist character. The structure was completed in co-operation with Dominik Merlini and Jan C. Kamsetzer in the early 19th century.

» It was along the amber route in Kruszwica on Lake Gopło that the first fortified settlement arose in the 8th century. It was one of the main strongholds of the Polanian state. The Romanesque collegiate of SS Peter and Paul dates from the period 1120-1140.

« Strzelno, one of the oldest localities in Poland, grew up round the cloister of the Norbertine Sisters. The Church of St Prokop, a Romanesque rotunda, was erected c. 1133-1160.

⌄ The original post-Norbertine Church of the Holy Trinity in Strzelno was built after 1175. In its main nave are found Romanesque columns displaying the personifications of the virtues and vices.

72

˅ The originally Romanesque Church of St John in Mogilno was rebuilt in the 15th and 16th centuries and again in 1760-1797. Two crypts have survived from the Romanesque period, one of which includes a reconstructed altar.

˅ The Baroque Church of the Assumption of the BVM in Trzemeszno was built in 1762-1781 round the walls of a Romanesque basilica from the early 12th century.

« In 1933, in the locality of Biskupin, 33 kilometres from Gniezno, the remains of a settlement dating from the Lusatian Culture of 16th-17th centuries BC was discovered.

» Gniezno Cathedral boasts two-winged bronze doors containing 18 bas relief scenes of the life and martyr's death of St Wojciech (Adalbert). They rank among the most splendid examples of Romanesque art in Poland.

74

«» Gniezno had served as the capital of the Polanian state. The first church was erected there before 970, the next -- a Romanesque structure -- in the 11th century. There Mieszko I buried his wife Dąbrówka. From there, St Wojciech set out on his last missionary expedition and there he was laid to rest. There too Poland's kings were crowned from 1025 until the 14th century.

MASOVIA

Masovia in the early Middle Ages belonged to the Masovian tribe. Mieszko I annexed that region to the Polanian state in the 10th century. But Masovia was not incorporated into the Kingdom of Poland until 1526. In 1596, Poland's capital was moved from Kraków to Warsaw, Masovia's principal city. The most characteristic feature of the Masovia's lowland landscape is the willow. Rows of them mark the borders of fields or flower-covered meadows.

» Weeping willows are a typical element of the Masovian landscape.

⌄ The mermaid monument - symbol of Warsaw.

« The Abbey of Regular Canons in Czerwińsk is situated on an escarpment overlooking the River Vistula. The Romanesque Church of the Assumption of the BVM is one of the Masovia region's most interesting architectural relics.

↳ The Renaissance-style Cathedral of the BVM in Płock, dating from 1532-1535, was erected on the relics of a Romanesque structure from the first half of the 12th century. It underwent further alterations down to the early 19th century. Its new façade, designed by Stefan Szyller,

≈» Łowicz is a town known for its characteristic folk costumes. Łowicz attire may be admired especially during Corpus Christi processions. The region's folk-crafts may be viewed at the local ethnographic museum. On display is an extensive collection of folk costumes, paper cuttings and wayside shrines. Examples of the region's wooden architecture may be seen at the skansen (open-air museum) in Maurzyce near Łowicz.

« A skansen, the Masovian Rural Museum, is found in Sierpc. It contains relics of folk architecture, including the country inn from Sochocin.

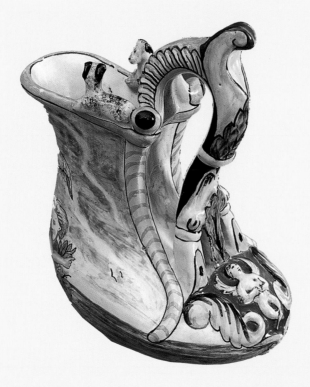

» The romantic scenic park in Arcadia was laid out at the behest of Princess Helena Radziwiłł in 1778.

« A majolica workshop operated at the Nieborów estate in 1881-1906. At present, copies of the works of a century ago are being produced there.

« In the library of Nieborów Palace stand 13 mahogany cupboards full of priceless books.

80

Nieborów Palace was built by Tylman of Gameren for Primate Michał Radziejowski in 1690-1696. After Nieborów was taken over by the Radziwiłłs, Helena Przeździecka-Radziwiłł had a romantic-sentimental park laid out in nearby Arkadia.

A statue of Cupid by Ethienne Maurice Falconet adorns the palace's staircase.

⌃ The environs of Nieborów are densely forested and include a superb birch-wood lane.

« A fortified church erected in Masovian Gothic style in 1551-1561 is found in Brochów. It was there that Fryderyk Chopin was baptised.

» The Gothic castle in Oporów was build for Gnizeno Archbishop Władysław Oporowski in c. 1440. Reconstructed in the 18th and 19th centuries, it regained its original shape following a conservation project in 1962-1965, whilst retaining its Baroque elements. Set on a quadrangular plan with an interior courtyard, it was surrounded by a moat. At present, it houses the Oporów Museum of period manorhouse interiors.

ʌ ↵ Żelazowa Wola is the birthplace of Fryderyk Chopin. All that remains of the former manor-house of Count Skarbek is the courtyard annexe, known as 'Chopin Manor', in which the composer was born in 1810. It now houses a biographical museum containing furnishings of the period. The manor is set in a sprawling park designed (1932-1937) by F. Krzywda Polkowski. Interesting species of trees and shrubs may be encountered there.

83

« The landscape in the vicinity of Żelazowa Wola abounds in willow-trees. They are most often planted along roads to provide shade for travellers.

84

⌃ The Gothic castle of the Dukes of Masovia on the River Łyna in Ciechanów was probably erected in 1427-1429 by stone-mason Niklos. Its height was subsequently increased on two occasions, and in 1657 it was destroyed by the invading Swedes. In disuse since the latter half of the 17th century, it was recently been made accessible to tourists. It houses a District Museum.

« The neo-Gothic palace in Opinogóra near Ciechanów was designed by Henryk Marconi and built after 1843. It was built for the outstanding poet of the Romantic period, Zygmunt Krasiński.

≍ Liw Castle was built in the late 14th century and served as the seat of the dukes of Masovia. At present, it houses a collection of old weapons and a gallery of portraits from the 18th and 19th c.

≋ The Gothic-Renaissance Basilica of the Annunciation of the BVM and St Matthew in Pułtusk was built in 1439-1449 and in the 1540s. Its main nave together with the presbytery is covered with cradle vaulting.

« In Gołąb on the Vistula, there stands a mannerist church dating from 1628-1636 and a House of Loretto with ceramic sculptures of the prophets, executed by Giovanni Anotnio Collombo.

« Castle Square took on its present shape at the start of the 19th century. Originally it had been the castle forecourt, studded with numerous structures, a remnant of which is the Gothic bridge.

⌁ The Royal Castle was built for King Zygmunt III Vasa after Poland's capital had been moved to Warsaw. The construction of a new residence on a pentagonal plan was entrusted to Italian architects, Giovanni Trevano, Giacomo Rodondo and Matteo Castelli. The castle underwent numerous renovations and expansion schemes in the centuries that followed. Burnt in 1939, its flame-gutted ruins were blown up in 1944. The castle was rebuilt through public donations in 1971-1984.

» The Royal Castle's Hall of Knights was built in 1781-1786 after a design by Dominik Merlini. It was decorated with the historical paintings of Marcello Bacciarelli and a statue of Chronos sculpted by Le Brun and Monaldi.

≽ The interior décor of the Royal Castle's Marble Room was created during the reign of King Władysław IV, the son of King Zygmunt III. During the castle's major renovation undertaken by King Stanisław August Poniatowski, a portrait gallery of Polish kings, painted by Marcello Bacciarelli, was added.

87

≫ The Old Town Market-place is the place most frequented by Warsaw inhabitants and visitors alike. It was created when the town became incorporated towards the end of the 13th century. Round its rim the town's wealthiest patricians built their homes.

≫ A monument to a Young Freedom-Fighter, sculpted by Jerzy Jarnuszkiewicz, adorns the Old Town walls. It commemorates the children and youths who took part in the 1944 Warsaw Uprising.

« The double portal of Wilczkowski House (No. 21 Marketplace) dates from 1608, when Warsaw Old Town Mayor Paweł Zembrzuski built his seat there. The 18th-century political reformer Hugo Kołłątaj had lived and died in the house.

⌃ Basilisk House, built in the 15th century, owes its name to the legend of a lizard whose gaze could kill. The monster died after gazing into one of the mirrors a young tailor had surrounded himself with.

» The Visitation Sisters' Baroque-style Church of St Joseph was the creation of Karol Bay in 1728-1733. Its unusual façade and interior were designed somewhat later by Efraim Schroeger. The main altar came from the workshop of Jan Jerzy Plersz. Many valuable paintings have been preserved in the church including Tadeusz Kuntze-Konicz's Visitaiton in the main altar and Daniel Szulc's St Louis Gonzaga.

⌄ Cobbler Jan Kiliński, a hero of the Kościuszko Insurrection, is portrayed by the 1936 monument of sculptor Stanisław Jackowski which stands in Podwale Street. Kiliński led the people of Warsaw in the uprising.

⌃ Architect Jan Zygmunt Deybel von Hammerau built a monumental palace for Jan Fryderyk Sapieha in 1731-1734. Its extremely decorative façade is adorned with rococo portals and window edging.

« The Monument to the Heroes of Warsaw, known as the Warsaw Nike, was created by Marian Konieczny. Unveiled in front of the Wielki Theatre in 1964, it has since been moved to the embankment overlooking the East-West Thoroughfare.

⌃ The classicist building of the Wielki Theatre was built in 1825-1833 according to a design by Antoni Corazzi, assisted by Ludwik Kozubowski. Originally known as the Narodowy (national) Theatre, owing to the political situation after the fall of the November Insurrection, its name was changed to Wielki (great) Theatre. It boasts Europe's biggest opera stage, can accommodate an audience of 1,900 and has played host to some of the world's greatest singers .

« The Ghetto Heroes' Memorial, the work of Marek Suzin and Natan Rappaport, forms part of the Trail of Jewish Martyrdom and Struggle. It was erected on the site of clashes between Jewish freedom-fighters and the Nazi Germans during the 1943.

≫ The Palace of Culture and Science was built in 1952-1955 according to the design of Lev Rudnev as a gift of the nations of the USSR to Warsaw. It is an example of socialist realist architecture. It is 234 metres tall.

≪ Ujazdów Castle, perched on the Vistula escarpment, was built on orders from King Zygmunt III Vasa in 1624.

⌃ The building of Warsaw Polytechnic was built in 1899-1901, chiefly by architect Stefan Szyller. Inside is a magnificent four-storey hall fringed with galleries and topped with a skylight.

93

» The zoological park covers an area of 40 hectares in right-bank Warsaw. It was established in 1928 and boasts 3,000 animals which may be viewed in outdoor runs. Rather original is the notion of exhibiting brown bears in a run adjacent to a busy street.

» The Palace on the Water is the principal building of Royal Łazienki Park. The original baths, designed by Tyman of Gameren, were built by Stanisław Herakliusz Lubomirski in about 1680. During the reign of King Stanisław August Poniatowski, a classicist palace designed by Dominik Merlini arose.

« During the building project, a former Baroque grotto at the centre of the building was remodelled. Marble statues of Polish kings are found in the rotunda's four niches.

 A 1909 secessionist-style monument to the outstanding Polish composer Fryderyk Chopin was unveiled in Łazienki Park in 1926. In summer, Sunday piano recitals are held at the foot of the monument.

94

ʌ The plafond in the Queen's Study, called the Chamber of Mirrors, was the work of Claude Callot and depicts Queen Maria Kazimiera Sobieska as Aurora.

95

« The oldest part of Wilanów Palace is its main hull. It was built according to a design by Augustyn Locci in 1681-1696 for Jan III Sobieski. In 1732-1729, wings on both sides of its forecourt were added. Work on the palace continued with interruptions until the end of the 19th century.

« Izrael K. Poznański's factory in Łódź from the latter half of the 19th century was built in the Rohbau style of bare brick not covered over with stucco.

» The ducal castle in Czersk was built in the 14th century as the seat of Masovian Duke Janusz I. After the Vistula changed its course and moved away from the town, the castle lost its strategic value, and the duke and his court moved to Warsaw.

« The palace of Izrael Kalman Poznański in Łódź at ulica Ogrodowa 15 was designed by Hilary Majewski. The monumental, neo-Baroque edifice, which underwent modifications until 1900, now houses the Łódź Municipal Museum. Its impressive interiors, full of gilded elements, stuccowork, panelling and mirrors, attest to the opulence for which the palaces of pre-war Łódź industrialists were known.

⌃ An Art Nouveau statue in the hall of Poznański's palace.

97

« Janowiec Castle, built for Piotr Firlej before 1537, took on its Baroque form during a renovation carried out by Santi Gucci and Tyman of Gameren.

« The Baroque palace in Puławy was built for Stanisław Herakliusz Lubomirski in 1676-1679 by Tylman of Gameren. During the Czartoryski era it was redesigned by Chrystian Piotr Aigner.

» Granaries in Kazimierz Dolny, of which there had originally been dozens, were erected along the Vistula. One of the surviving ones is the Ulatowski Granary from 1591.

⌃ The environs of Kazimierz Dolny abound in picturesque hills and ravines. A rural lane leads along one such ravine to a nearby locality.

» A splendid attic adorns Celejów House in Kazimierz Dolny, built in the early 17th century.

« Kazimierz Dolny is a town of painters and writers. Its charming narrow streets and beautiful scenery that can be admired from the rolling hills attract throngs of tourists.

99

WARMIA AND MASURIA

North-western Poland, known as the 'land of a thousand lakes', is the ideal place for those who yearn for nature uncontaminated by industry. Especially worth visiting is the Suwałki region, whose virgin backwaters await tourists.

» Lake Omulec in Masuria.

⌄ Sailing-boat regattas are often held on the Masurian lakes.

⌃ The flood waters of the River Biebrza constitute Europe's biggest wetlands. Biebrza National Park, created to protect this area, is Poland's largest.

« The Branicki Park and Palace Complex in Białystok is a late-Baroque work of Tylman of Gameren from 1691-1697.

A skansen of north-eastern Polish wooden architecture has been established near Jurowce. Among the buildings on display is a windmill from the vicinity of Tykocin dating from 1836.

↗ In Wigry on Monastery Point (formerly an island), a Camedulian monastery complex was built in 1694-1745 by P. Putini.

» The bridge over the River Błędzianka in Stańczyki was built in 1926 to accommodate a railway line then being developed. Today, the 31.5-metre-high structure serves as a place for bungee-jumping.

The Jesuit monastery complex in Święta Lipka was erected at the turn of the 18th century. According to legend, round 1300 the Blessed Mother and Infant Jesus appeared on a linden-tree growing at the spot. This Baroque church is a galleried basilica with a twin-tower façade. A quadrangle of galleries with corner turrets encases the church. The turrets are decorated with Baroque-style sculptures from 1774-1748, the work of Krzysztof Perwanger of Tolmicko, and mural paintings created by Maciej Jan Mayer in 1722-1737.

» Remnants of Gothic town walls have survived in Nowe Miasto. Its most interesting elements is Stork's Gate, at the top of which -- in accordance with its name -- a stork has made its nest.

⌄ The castle in Lidzbark Warmiński has a square, galleried forecourt. The castle houses the Warmia Museum with a collection of religious art from the Gothic to Baroque as well as late-19th and 20th-century Polish paintings.

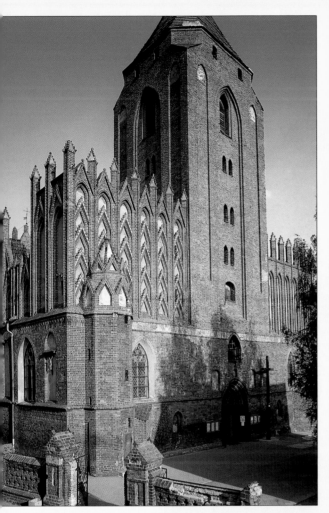

The Church of St John the Baptist and St John the Evangelist in Orneta is from the latter half of the 14th century. The pride of this Gothic church is the lacework attic with alternating blind windows and pinnacles. Its external walls are decorated with a frieze featuring a row of figures in arcades.

» The skansen in Olsztynek was set up in 1938. It contains a collection of wooden peasant architecture brought in from various parts of Warmia, Masuria, Powiśle, Sambia, Bracja and Prussian Lithuania. Apart from peasant cottages, outbuildings and beehives, the most interesting structures are the wind-mills and an arcaded, half-timbered inn.

107

The fortified cathedral complex in Frombork was erected in the 13th century as the seat of the Warmia Chapter. Standing 20 metres above the Vistula Lagoon, it was surrounded by defensive walls that included watchtowers and a formidable main gate. It was there that Mikołaj Kopernik worked from 1512 to 1516, and again from 1522 until his death. Built in 1342-1388, Frombork Cathedral is Warmia's biggest Gothic church. Striking stellar vaulting is found in its interior.

» A stud farm is found in Kadyny on the shore of the Vistula Lagoon. Holidays in the saddle are organised there, and the local ravine-dissected hills encourage visitors to take britzka tours.

The Gothic hall-type Church of St Catherine in Braniewo was erected in stages from 1346 to 1442. Following its total destruction in 1945, it has recently been rebuilt from the ground up. The interior contains superb stellar vaulting and two Gothic triptychs: St Ann from the start of the 16th century and the Blessed Virgin from 1430.

» The Church of St Nicholas in Elbląg was built in stages from 1240 to 1511. In 1598, a Renaissance dome was added to its tall tower that rises above the city. The church interior contains interesting Gothic relics: figures of the Apostles from 1400-1414 and a crucifix from the beginning of the 15th century.

POMERANIA

Pomerania is a region lying between the Lower Odra and Vistula, the Baltic, the River Noteć and the Lower Warta. Historically, it has been divided into East Pomerania, whose main city is Gdańsk, and West Pomerania centred round Szczecin. The region has been shaped by the passage of glaciers which left behind small lakes such as those of the Drawsko Lake District and picturesque hills situated mainly in what is known as Kashubian Switzerland.

» In the summer, the place in Poland most frequented by tourists is the Baltic coast. Its wide, sandy beaches stretching along the country's entire northern frontier are a particular attraction.

⩦ Fishing is a well-developed industry on the Baltic. Fishermen have large fishing boats fitted with the latest equipment. Fishing boats pulled up on shore and nets drying in the sun are things of the past.

Situated along the River Vistula, the town of Toruń was established in 1233 by the Teutonic Knights. It was then that today's Old Town was built, followed by the castle and New Town. Toruń, a town of well-to-do merchants, rebelled against the Teutonic Order's authority in 1454 and placed itself under the rule of Poland's kings.

⌃ In Szeroka Street, the main promenade of Toruń, one can purchase honey-spice cakes (gingerbread).

« A mediaeval privy known as 'gdanisko' is the only fragment of the 13th-century Teutonic Knights' castle to survive in its entirety.

⌃ In front of the town hall stands a monument of Miko-łaj Kopernik (Copernicus), sculpted by Friedrich Tieck in 1853. Kopernik proved the correctness of the heliocentric theory.

⌃ Of the fortified walls that once encir-cled Toruń little more has survived than a stretch of fortifications along the Vistula. The best known of the four bas-tions is the Leaning Tower.

« The town hall in Toruń's Old Town is one of Europe's most magnificent exam-ples of mediaeval burgher architecture.

The Gothic castle at Golub Dobrzyń was built at the turn of the 15th century for the Teutonic Knights. Its Renaissance attic was added when the castle was being converted into the residence of Anna Vasa.

⤢⤡ Gothic Kwidzyn Caslte was built in 1320-1347 by the Teutonic Order and was the chapter seat. One of its interesting elements is a privy to which an arcade-mounted passageway leads.

» One of the oldest churches in the Chełmno region is the Shrine of the Holy Trinity in Chełmża. Built in stages in 1251-1291 and in the 14th century, it is a three-nave church topped by stellar vaulting. Apart from the predominantly Baroque and Rococo interior décor, several earlier treasures have survived: two Gothic sculptures of the Crucifixion and the Renaissance tombstone of Bishop Piotr Kostka.

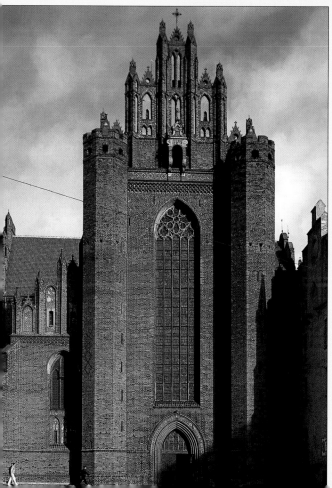

The former Cistercian monastic complex in Pelpin was founded in 1258. The imposing Church of the BVM was erected between the end of the 13th century to the latter half of the 14th. Its richly sculpted entrance portal from c. 1300 contains a neo-Romanesque tympanum.

⌃ The most magnificent fortress in Polish territory stands in Malbork on the River Nogat. From 1280 it served as the seat of the commander of the Order of Teutonic Knights and after 1309 it became the capital of the Teutonic state. Construction began with High Castle, after 1310 Middle Castle was erected, and in 1382-1399 the Palace of the Grand Master was built. Following the defeat of the Teutonic Order at Grunwald, the castle complex did not fall into Polish hands until 1457.

« The amber office may be viewed at a exhibition entitled 'The Annals of Amber'.

« The Summer Refectory in the Grand Master's Palace is the most magnificent interior of Malbork Castle. It was there the Grand Master of the Teutonic Order received distinguished visitors. Embedded above the fireplace is a fragment of a stone cannon-ball -- a memento of the castle's siege by Polish-Lithuanian forces in 1410.

⌄ The forecastle, also known as the Low Castle, was built in the first half of the 14th century as the castle's utility premises. It contained workshops, an armoury, granaries and stables. That area was safeguarded by a protective wall and numerous towers like those pictured here: the Vice-Starost's Tower and the Administrator's Tower.

⌃ The Palace of the Grand Masters was built onto Malbork Castle on the River Nogat side. Work began in the first half of the 14th century, and the structure was expanded in 1383-1393. That was when the superb halls containing the Summer and Winter Refectory came into being.

» The bridge leading to the Middle Castle protected the access to the High Castle.

˅ A permanent exhibition featuring typical period artefacts has been set up in the convent's kitchen and bakery.

˄ A superb galleried staircase leads to the first floor of the High Castle.

« An exhibition of Gothic sculpture has been set up in the chambers of the High Castle. Included is a 15th-century Pieta.

⌃ The 1504 altar from Thecla in Sambii occupies a place of honour at the exhibition of Gothic sculpture in the High Castle.

⌃ The courtyard of Malbork's High Castle came into being in the 13th and early 14th centuries when three wings were added to the structure. The well, dug in the Middle Ages, had a depth of 18 metres.

« A fragment of the Golden Gate leading to St Ann's Chapel in the High Castle.

⌃ The pole-wall church with a brick presbytery in Stegna was built in 1681-1683.

« This arcaded house, characteristic of the Żuławy delta area was built in Krzywe Koło at the start of the 19th century.

Kashubian Ethnographic Park in the village of Wdzydze Kiszewskie was established in 1907 and is Poland's oldest skansen (open-air museum).

ⵣ A folk sculpture portraying the Madonna and Infant at the skansen in Wdzydze Kiszewskie.

» Kashubian Switzerland, situated south-east of Gdańsk, is known for its hilly morainic terrain dotted with numerous lakes.

» Długi Targ in Gdańsk runs from Green Gate on the River Motława to the town hall. There the town's most important secular structures are found: The Main Town Hall, Artus Manor and the most elegant town-houses.

⌃ The Great Council Chamber, known as the Red Hall, is the town hall's most beautiful interior. Its décor, created in the period from 1593 to 1608, was the work of Dutch and Gdańsk masters: Hans Vredeman de Vries, Izaak van den Blocke and Simon Herle.

» Artus Manor, dating from 1478-1481, was once the meeting place of the town's better-to-do burghers who espoused the principles of King Arthur's Knights of the Round Table. Its façade was rede-signed in 1616-1817 by Abraham van den Blocke.

« The Fountain of Neptune, the god of the sea and navigation, was erected in front of the town hall in Długi Targ (Long Market) in 1633 as a symbol of the town's prosper-ity.

« The River Motława, on whose banks Old Town is situated, is Gdańsk's principal waterway. During Gdańsk Days, sailing ships from all over the world converge on this Baltic port.

» Oliwa Cathedral was erected in the 13th century by the Cistercians who were first brought there in 1186. In the 17th and 18th centuries it was richly embellished to include such things as a symbolic sarcophagus of the Dukes of Pomerania as well as portraits of Polish princes and kings.

ˇ St Mary's Church in Gdańsk is Europe's biggest mediaeval brick church. It is a three-nave structure with a transept and a wreath of chapels, built in Gothic style in 1343-1502.

The figure of a warrior adorns the elevation of Gdańsk's manneristist Armoury.

The seashore part of Kępa Redłowska, which rises to an height of 91 metres above sea-level, is a scenic reserve. A mixed forest dominated by beech grows atop its steep cliff.

↳ The former Abbot's Palace in Oliwa, built in 1754-1756, today serves as the National Museum's gallery of contemporary art.

⌃ Slovincian National Park, established in 1967, has been included among World Biosphere Reserves. Its main attraction are shifting sand dunes rising to a height of 42 metres and changing their position by up to nine metres a year.

« Kamień Pomorski is a locality lying along Kamień Lagoon. In the early Middle Ages it had been a fortified Slavonic port town. It was there that the first Pomeranian coins were struck in the 12th century.

⌃ Poland's coastline is 528 kilometres long. Its many seaside resorts attract throngs of tourists, especially in summer.

⌄ St Mary's Church in Stargard Szczeciński was built towards the end of the 13th century. Its presbytery, wreath of chapels and twin-spired façade emerged during the church's 15th-century expansion. Remnants of Gothic murals have survived inside.

⌃ The late-Romanesque church in Kołbacz was erected in 1210-1239. The lion's share of the surviving structure dates from the church's Gothic reconstruction carried out in the first half of the 14th century.

↟ Loitz House is the most interesting relic of burgher architecture in Szczecin, the capital of West Pomerania. It was built in 1574 in the late-Gothic style for a wealthy banking family.

↡ The Gothic Church of SS Peter and Paul in Szczecin dates from 1470-1480. The mascarons adorning its exterior portray such Szczecin townsfolk as merchants, porters and fishermen.

The Old Town of Stargard Szczeciński is surrounded by a complex of mediaeval fortifications which include three gates: Pyrzyce Gate, Rampart Gate and Mill Gate (pictured).